# NIGHT SKY WATCHER

D0530526

To Kamini, Vikas and Sachin
– RP

Words in **bold** are explained
in the glossary on page 114

**Project Editor:** Tasha Percy
**Editorial Director:** Victoria Garrard
**Art Director:** Laura Roberts-Jensen

**For cobalt id**
**Editor:** Marek Walisiewicz
**Designers:** Darren Bland, Rebecca Johns and Paul Reid

Copyright © QED Publishing 2014

First published in the UK in 2014 by
QED Publishing
A Quarto Group company
The Old Brewery,
6 Blundell Street,
London, N7 9BH

www.qed-publishing.co.uk

All rights reserved. No part of this publication may be
reproduced, stored in a retrieval system, or transmitted in
any form or by any means, electronic, mechanical,
photocopying, recording, or otherwise, without the prior
permission of the publisher, nor be otherwise circulated
in any form of binding or cover other than that in which
it is published and without a similar condition being
imposed on the subsequent purchaser.

A catalogue record for this book is available from the
British Library.

ISBN 978 1 78171 657 1

Printed in China

# NIGHT SKY WATCHER

## RAMAN PRINJA

QED Publishing

# Contents

Get to grips with the motion of the planets and understand why the stars and constellations seem to move from one night to the next.

Find out what equipment you need to watch the night sky comfortably and safely.

Binoculars will help, but you don't need them to explore the night sky.

# Night Sky Essentials

Discover why some stars appear bright or coloured, while others are dim.

Learn the differences between stars, planets, galaxies and other objects in the sky.

# What can you see?

On a clear night the sky is decorated with a fantastic display of objects. You may be able to see **stars** of different colours, bright **planets** and a stunning **Moon**. Sometimes you'll be lucky enough to see a rare event such as a **meteor** shower, a **comet** or an **eclipse**.

## STAR OR PLANET?

The planets will usually be much brighter than most of the stars in the same area of the sky. The planets also don't twinkle as much as the stars. If you follow a planet over many nights, you should see that its position in the sky at the same time each night changes when compared to the stars.

Did you know?

Stars seem to twinkle in the night sky. This isn't because they get brighter and fainter, but because the air above us moves around and distorts their light before it reaches our eyes.

# SPOTTING OBJECTS

The best thing about night sky watching is that everyone can do it. All you need are your eyes or some simple binoculars, and this book.

The Sun ▲

## ASTROFACTS

>> Our nearest star is the Sun, which is 150 **million** kilometres away.

>> The next nearest star to us is called Proxima Centauri. It is 40 **trillion** kilometres away – that's 40 with 12 zeros on the end!

◄ Mercury

## LIGHTS IN THE SKY

Nearly all the tiny lights you see in the night sky are stars. Sometimes a planet may be in view. Mercury, Venus, Mars, Saturn and Jupiter are the only planets that can be seen with an unaided eye. On a very dark and clear night, you may be able to see another galaxy – a vast but very distant collection of **billions** of stars.

# Stars, planets and galaxies

When you look up at the night sky, most of the twinkling lights you see are stars. So what are stars, and what makes them different to planets, **galaxies** and other objects in the sky?

## WHAT ARE STARS?

Stars are giant balls of gas. Most of the gas is **hydrogen** – the simplest of all the **elements**. The gas is squeezed together so tightly, and gets so hot, that it triggers a process called **nuclear fusion**. This releases huge amounts of energy, including the light that we can see from trillions of kilometres away.

## WHAT ARE PLANETS?

When stars form, the edges of the **dust** clouds around them can clump together to form planets. Some planets are rocky, while others are made of gases or liquids. Jupiter, for example, is made mainly of hydrogen and **helium** gas.

Jupiter ▲

## WHAT ARE GALAXIES?

Galaxies are enormous collections of stars, dust and gas held together by gravity. Some contain trillions of stars and a few can be seen with the naked eye as faint smudges. Our Sun is part of a galaxy called the **Milky Way**.

▼ M101, The Pinwheel Galaxy

**Did you know?**

There are eight planets, including Earth, that go around our Sun. They formed about 4.5 billion years ago. New planets are still forming today around other stars.

Mercury ▶

Venus ▶

Earth ▶

Mars ▶

# Star watching

If your eyesight is very good, and it's a really clear night, you should be able to see more than 2000 individual stars – if you have the patience to count them! Take a closer look and you'll see that they aren't all the same, but differ in their brightness and colour.

## BRIGHT AND DIM STARS

Stars can appear bright because they are large and give out lots of light, or because they are closer to Earth than other stars. The brightest star in the night sky is called Sirius A, or the Dog Star. Another star, Rigel, is much bigger than Sirius A and gives out more light. But Sirius A looks brighter because it is 100 times closer to us.

◄ Sirius A

Rigel ►

▼ Supernova

## Imagine this

A supernova can release more energy in a few days than our Sun will give out over its whole life. You need to be very lucky to witness a supernova explosion – in our galaxy this event can be seen once every few hundred years.

## THE LIFE OF STARS

Stars are born inside giant clouds of dust and gas called **nebulae**. The dust and gas clump together, growing into dense, hot masses. Once these grow big enough, nuclear fusion begins and the star begins to shine. Stars also die as they use up their hydrogen fuel. Some shrink away, while others explode violently into **supernovae** and form **black holes**.

▲ Sharpless 2-106 nebula

## COLOURFUL STARS

Stars appear as tiny spots of light, but they don't all have the same colour. There are red, blue and yellow stars. Their colours are different because some stars are cooler (the red ones) and others are much hotter (blue ones).

### Did you know?

All the stars you can see with your naked eye are part of our galaxy – the Milky Way. There are more than 200 billion stars in the Milky Way and about 100 billion other galaxies in the Universe.

▲ Nebulae are giant star factories and look amazing through powerful **telescopes**.

# Patterns in the sky

With so many objects in the night sky, how do you find your way around? How can you tell which star is which? The answer is to look for the patterns made by the stars. These patterns stay the same from one night to the next making them great signposts in the sky.

Pleiades ▼

## STAR CLUSTERS

Some star patterns exist because their stars are close to each other and were born around the same time. You can see some of these **star clusters**, such as the Pleiades (or Seven Sisters), with your naked eye. They look even better through binoculars.

## IMAGINED PATTERNS

Most of the star patterns you can see in the sky are imagined. The shapes — such as animals or objects — result from the chance alignment of stars that are not related in any way and may in fact be hundreds of **light-years** apart. These patterns are called **constellations**.

◀ Ancient people thought that their gods fought battles in the sky.

## Did you know?

Most of the constellations were made up a long time ago by ancient Greek and Arab explorers. The constellations were named after the shapes of animals, gods or other figures in their myths and stories.

# THINGS TO DO

It's fun to look at a star-filled sky and invent your own constellation. First make a small picture frame from cardboard – about 10 by 10 centimetres. Hold the frame at arm's length and look through it, moving around the sky until you find a group of bright stars that fall within it. Try to imagine a shape by joining lines between five or seven stars in the frame. You could picture an animal or an object. What would you call your new constellation? See if you can find your constellation a few nights later.

▲ The Plough

# The constellations

With a little practice, you'll soon learn how to recognize the shapes and patterns in the sky, known as constellations. Spotting well-known constellations will help you get your bearings and move between objects in the sky.

## YOUR GUIDES TO THE SKY

There are 88 constellations used today to map out the sky. If you live north of the **equator**, you can see about 60 constellations; if you are in Earth's Southern **Hemisphere** you can see about 30. Some can be seen from almost anywhere in the world. This picture shows the shapes of just a few of the constellations you might see in the night sky.

Pisces ►

◄ Crux

◄ Gemini

◄ Taurus

◄ Aquarius

## CONSTELLATIONS IN VIEW

You can't see all 88 constellations at the same time. Which ones you can see depends on where you are on Earth's surface, the season of the **year** and the time of night.

## LOOKALIKE?

Some of the constellations do look like the thing they are named after – the constellation Leo (the Latin word for 'Lion'), for example, does resemble a lion. But does the pair of stars in the constellation Canes Venatici ('The Hunting Dogs') really look like a pair of dogs?

Leo ▲

Canes Venatici ▲

Virgo ▶

Lynx ▶

▲ Aquila

Scorpius ▶

◀ Carina

Ursa Major ▶

Stars seem to move ▶
around in the sky.

# The moving sky

Once you can recognize the shape of a few constellations, pick one and try following it over a few hours. Check its position once every 30 minutes or so and you should notice that it seems to move across the sky. But it's not the sky that's moving – it's our planet, Earth!

## SPINNING EARTH

Imagine a giant rod that passes through Earth, from the North **Pole** to the South Pole. Just like a spinning top, Earth spins on this rod (or axis). It makes one full turn every day. As Earth turns, some parts receive the light of the Sun, while others are dark. That's what gives us night and **day**. As Earth turns, the stars in the night sky – just like the Sun in the daytime sky – seem to move slowly.

Sun ▶

◀······ Day

◀ Earth

Night ⠇

◀······ Axis

## STAR TRAILS

If you watch the stars over a few hours, you'll see that they seem to rotate around one point in the sky. This is the top of the imaginary rod that passes through Earth's poles. You can see how they rotate in a photograph which was taken over a few hours.

## CONSTANT SHAPES

Even though the stars seem to move across the sky, the patterns of the constellations stay the same. The spacing you see between groups of stars doesn't change. A constellation may rise, move above you, turn sideways or even upside down, but it won't spread apart or change shape.

Did you know?

In the Northern Hemisphere, the top of the imaginary rod passing through Earth's poles points towards a star called Polaris. This is also called the North Star because it always shows which way is north.

5pm ▶

8pm ▶

11pm ▶

◀ How the constellation Cassiopeia seems to move over one night.

2am ▶

◀ 5am

# Our changing view

Not only do the stars seem to move during the course of one night, they also seem to shift from one month to the next. This is because the Earth **orbits** the Sun, bringing different constellations into view at different times of year.

## A YEAR IN ORBIT

Our planet takes one year to complete a single **orbit** of the Sun. We can only see stars at night, because they are too faint to spot during daylight. As Earth moves around the Sun, the stars we can see at night change very slowly from one day to the next. You'll notice the change if you look up at the same part of the sky at the same time of night every month.

▼ Viewpoint

◄ Earth

▼ In 1530, the Polish scientist Nicolaus Copernicus was the first to argue that the Earth orbited the Sun.

▲ These constellations can be seen in January.

The distances between stars are so ▶ huge that scientists don't measure them in kilometres. Instead, they measure them in **light-years**. One light-year is the distance that a flash of light would travel in a year. It is equal to about 9.5 trillion kilometres.

Background of stars

Viewpoint ▼

Earth's orbit

◀ Sun

▲ The constellations you can see from one point on Earth change slowly throughout the year.

▲ These constellations can be seen in June.

# Finding your way

The stars seem to move in the night sky in complicated ways. So how can you find your way around? The easiest way is to look for star patterns, or constellations, and use them to point the way to other objects in the sky. You can also use a simple tool called a **planisphere**.

## GET YOUR BEARINGS

In this book, you'll read that a star can be seen in the north or in the west. So, you'll need a simple compass to know which way you are facing. The needle of the compass always points north.

## STAR-HOPPING

Some of the constellations have very clear shapes and are easy to spot in the sky — especially when you have learned to recognize their outlines. Once you've found these 'easy' constellations, you can draw imaginary lines between their stars. Following these lines will guide you to other nearby constellations, stars and even galaxies. This is called star-hopping and you can start doing this on page 28.

The North ▶
Star

◀ The Plough

Imaginary
line

▲ Extending an imaginary
line from the two
stars in The Plough
will point your way to
The North Star.

## MEASURING DISTANCE

If you need to describe how far one star appears to be from another, try using your hand! Looking at the sky, stretch out your arm as far as it will go. The width of your hand — or finger — is a quick and convenient measure of the relative distance between stars in the night sky.

# PLANISPHERE
### Latitude 40° North

NORTH

Eastern Horizon

Western Horizon

NOVEMBER

OCTOBER

DECEMBER

SEPTEMBER

JANUARY

MIDNIGHT

11 PM
10 PM
9 PM
8 PM
7 PM
6 PM
5 PM
4 PM
3 PM
2 PM
1 PM
NOON
11 AM

1 AM
2 AM
3 AM
4 AM
5 AM
6 AM

APRIL

MAY

Set the date and time ▶ on the scale on the edge of the planisphere

## USING A PLANISPHERE

A planisphere is a simple way of seeing which constellations are in view on a particular day and time. It is made of a circular plastic disc with an oval window cut into it. Underneath the plastic is a map of the stars and constellations. Turning the plastic disc to set the time and date will reveal the visible sky within the oval window.

# Getting prepared

Choosing the right time and place to watch the night sky will make all the difference to how much you see. Pick a clear night so that clouds don't block your view – and get ready with some simple kit.

## WHERE TO WATCH

Find a safe, dark place close to home. Gardens are great, but only if they are well away from the lights of your house or street lights, which will spoil your view. Try a local park or playground, but always make sure you are supervised by an adult.

## SPOTTING STARS

Wait about 10 minutes to let your eyes get used to the darkness – you'll see a lot more stars.

## KEEP WARM AND COMFORTABLE

Don't forget to wear warm clothes and a hat. Even spring and summer nights can become chilly. You'll be staring at the sky most of the time, so get comfortable. Lying back on a deckchair or a waterproof ground sheet will let you look up without straining your neck.

▼ Moonless nights are best for stargazing – that's because the bright light reflected from the Moon makes it harder to see fainter stars and planets.

## Did you know ?

Your eyes are more sensitive to faint light when you don't look directly at an object. So when you're struggling to see a distant star, look just slightly to one side of it.

## THINGS TO DO

Take a small torch and wrap a red plastic sweet wrapper around its light. Keep it in place with a rubber band. Using this red light outside will let you read this book and see where you're going without spoiling your night vision.

# Seeing more

Using just your eyes, you'll be able to see stars, trace the shapes of the constellations in the sky, spot meteors, and follow the movements of five planets. But add a pair of binoculars and you'll be able to see faint stars, look at details on the Moon's surface, and even make out the moons of the planet Jupiter.

## BINOCULARS

You may already have a pair of binoculars at home. They're great for watching the night sky because they're light and always ready for action. If you're planning on asking for a pair as a present, look for ones marked 7 x 50 or 10 x 50. The first number gives their magnification and the second number tells you the **diameter** of the main lens in millimeters. The wider this lens, the more light it can gather to make faint stars seem brighter.

## THINGS TO DO

Why not hold a star party? Invite your friends and family over on a dark, clear night and use your know-how to guide them through the wonders of the Moon, stars, and planets!

# THINGS TO DO

The best way to learn the patterns of stars in the night sky is to draw them using a pencil and paper. First, choose an area of the sky. Draw large dots for the brightest stars in that area, then fill in fainter stars as smaller dots. Make notes about what you see – some stars have a red or blue colour, for example.

Red star

Bright blue star

## KEEP STEADY

When you use binoculars, the stars may appear to wobble. That's because binoculars magnify any movement of your hands. Try resting the binoculars on a fence or bracing them on your knees to keep them steady.

**Find your way around the night sky using familiar pointer stars.**

**Explore the constellations and trace out shapes of monsters and heroes in the sky.**

**Spot distant stars, galaxies, giant dust clouds and other exotic objects by 'hopping' around the constellations.**

# Star-hopping

Get to know the names of the stars and constellations.

Learn how to find the North Star and you'll never get lost again!

# Orion

Orion ('The Hunter') is one of the easiest patterns to identify in the sky. Two of the brightest ten stars seen at night are in this constellation.

## BETELGEUSE

This star is a red **supergiant**, more than 650 times the size of the Sun.

## MAIN STARS

Orion is made up of seven main stars called Betelgeuse, Rigel, Bellatrix, Saiph, Alnitak, Alnilam and Mintaka.

## ORION'S BELT

Alnitak, Alnilam and Mintaka make up the belt of Orion the Hunter.

## RIGEL

This star is a rare blue supergiant that shines 100,000 times more powerfully than the Sun.

# SPOTTING ORION

If you live in the Northern Hemisphere, Orion is easy to find in winter. Face southeast and look up halfway between the horizon and overhead. You should spot three bright stars close together in an almost straight line. These make up Orion's Belt. Head upwards from the belt and you'll come to a bright, reddish star called Betelgeuse, which marks the shoulder of the Hunter. Head down and south from the belt stars to a bright blue star, Rigel. It marks Orion's left foot.

◀ Orion's shape was imagined to be a hunter holding a club in one hand and a shield in the other.

▼ Orion Nebula

## Did you know?

A huge star-making factory called the Orion Nebula is located just below Orion's Belt.

# Star-hopping
## to Canis Major

Once you've found Orion, you can use it as a
signpost to find the nearby constellation of Canis
Major ('The Great Dog'). This includes the brightest
star in the night sky – Sirius – as well as five other
very bright stars that make its dog-like shape.

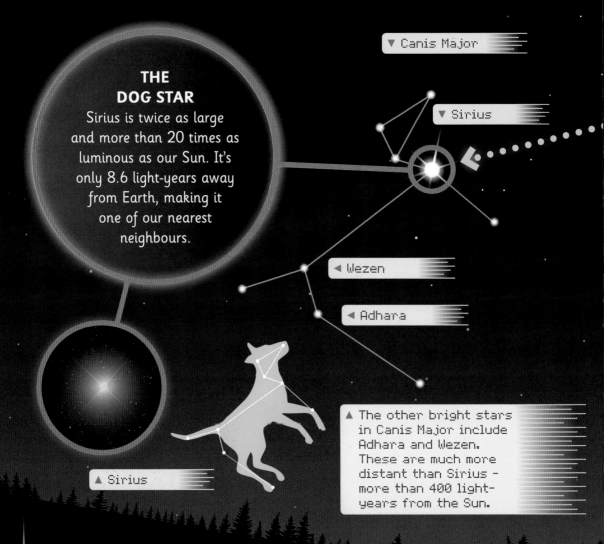

**▼ Canis Major**

**▼ Sirius**

**THE DOG STAR**
Sirius is twice as large
and more than 20 times as
luminous as our Sun. It's
only 8.6 light-years away
from Earth, making it
one of our nearest
neighbours.

◀ Wezen

◀ Adhara

▲ The other bright stars
in Canis Major include
Adhara and Wezen.
These are much more
distant than Sirius –
more than 400 light-
years from the Sun.

▲ Sirius

Sirius was known to the ancient Egyptians as the Nile Star. When it could be seen in the morning before sunrise, it was a sign that the great River Nile was about to flood.

▲ Orion

The River Nile ▲ during a flood

## HOPPING TO CANIS MAJOR

Find the three stars of Orion's Belt. Now draw an imaginary line through the belt and down towards the horizon. Follow this line and you will easily spot a very bright star called Sirius. Sirius is in the constellation of Canis Major ('The Great Dog'), and Sirius itself is sometimes called the dog star!

# Star-hopping
## to Taurus and the Seven Sisters

Orion ▼

Using Orion's Belt as a pointer in the sky, it is easy to find the constellation of Taurus ('The Bull'). Nearby, look out for a beautiful jewel-like cluster of stars called the Seven Sisters.

### HOPPING TO TAURUS

Draw an imaginary line through the belt of Orion and follow it upwards through Orion's shield. You'll soon reach a small group of stars that make a 'V' shape. This marks the start of the horns and face of Taurus – the Bull.

▼ Crab Nebula

◄ Using a pair of binoculars, look just above the lower horn of the bull, next to the star called Zeta Tauri. You may see a white smudge. This is the Crab Nebula, the remains of a star that exploded as a supernova in July 1054.

▼ Taurus

◄ Crab Nebula

◄ Zeta Tauri

## SEVEN SISTERS
If you carry on up along the line from the belt of Orion, past Aldebaran, you'll come to a small group of stars, about one thumb width across at arm's length, called the Pleiades (also known as the 'Seven Sisters').

Aldebaran ►

## ALDEBARAN
Look for the bright orange star on the left horn of the 'V' of Taurus. This star is called Aldebaran and it marks the eye of the bull. It is an old giant star that has spread outwards.

Seven Sisters ►

◄ Aldebaran and Taurus constellation

# The Plough

High in the sky in spring and summer, you can see one of the most famous of all star patterns – 'The Plough'. This pattern of seven stars is actually the brightest part of a much bigger constellation called Ursa Major – 'The Great Bear'.

Mizar ▶

▲ Alioth

Megrez ▲

▲ Alkaid

Phecda ▶

**HANDLE**
The stars that make the handle of the saucepan shape in the Plough are Alkaid, Mizar and Alioth.

## SPOTTING THE PLOUGH

The Plough is visible all year round in the Northern Hemisphere. Some people call it 'the saucepan', because it seems to make the shape of a pot with a handle. The Plough is made up of seven bright stars. In the middle of summer, you'll easily see it in the northern part of the night sky. Try to find the 'handle' of the saucepan first and then spot the stars that make up the pot shape. Holding your hand at arms length, the Plough is about two full hands across.

◀ Powerful telescopes have shown that Bode's Galaxy has a **spiral** shape, like our galaxy, the Milky Way.

## SPOTTING BODE'S GALAXY

It's hard to see other galaxies with your naked eye. But with a pair of binoculars, you should be able to spot Bode's Galaxy. It looks like a blurry patch over the Great Bear's shoulders.

▼ Dubhe

◀ Merak

### ASTROFACTS

>> The stars in the Plough are about 75 to 125 light-years away from Earth.

>> The Plough is so well known that it has different names in different countries. In India, it's called 'The Seven Sages' and in China 'The Northern Ladle'.

**SAUCEPAN**
The pot of the saucepan is made up of four stars – Megrez, Phecda, Merak and Dubhe.

# Star-hopping
## to Ursa Minor and the North Star

Knowing the stars of the Plough will help you find the nearby constellation of Ursa Minor ('The Little Bear') and locate the North Star. This star, also called Polaris, is directly over Earth's North Pole. So, if you face Polaris, you'll know that you're facing north.

Ancient navigators ▶ used instruments like this quadrant to measure the position of the North Star and so find their location, even when they were sailing the oceans far away from any landmarks.

▼ The Plough

Merak ▶

## THINGS TO DO

The North Star not only shows you which direction is north, but it also tells you how far you are from Earth's equator. Stretch out both of your arms. Point one at the North Star and one at the horizon below it. The angle between your arms tells you your **latitude**. If you are at the equator, it will be zero (your arms will be together); if you are at the North Pole, it will be 90 degrees (a right angle).

An angle of ▲ 50 degrees means you are about the latitude of London.

Ursa Minor ▲

## URSA MINOR

The North Star is part of the constellation called Ursa Minor. Its shape is a bit like that of The Plough, but it is smaller and much fainter in the sky. See if you can make out its shape after you've found the pole star.

## HOPPING TO THE NORTH STAR

Find the two stars – Dubhe and Merak – at the front of the 'cooking pot' of The Plough. Draw an imaginary line between them and upwards. Move along this line about five times the distance between Dubhe and Merak and you'll arrive at the pole star, Polaris.

## POLARIS

Other stars seem to move around in the sky, but Polaris stays fixed in the same position. This made it a great help to ancient navigators and explorers.

# Star-hopping to Leo

The stars of the Plough can be used to find the constellation of Leo ('The Lion'). Leo is one of the few constellations that really looks like what it is supposed to show, so look out for the lion in the night sky!

## THE TERRIFYING LION

In Greek myth, Leo was a fearsome lion that terrorized the people of Nemea. Its skin was so tough that no one could kill it with a sword or spear. The lion was finally killed by the hero Hercules, who strangled it to death.

## THE LEONIDS

Every November a shower of meteors called the Leonids seems to stream out from the region of the constellation Leo. The meteors burn up as they streak through Earth's **atmosphere**, producing a fantastic firework display overhead.

## HOPPING TO LEO

You can easily see Leo in spring in the Northern Hemisphere and in autumn in the Southern Hemisphere. First find the stars Megrez and Phecda in the Plough. Follow a line between these stars towards the horizon. You'll come to a bright blue-white star called Regulus, which is in the constellation Leo.

▼ The Plough

◀ Megrez

## ALGIEBA

After Regulus, the second brightest star in the constellation is Algieba. Scientists think that it is orbited by a huge planet at least twice the size of Jupiter.

▼ Denebola

▼ Algieba

◀ Leo

▲ Regulus

Look at the stars around ▲ Regulus. Notice that they make a shape like a back-to-front question mark, with Regulus at the bottom of the question mark.

# Cassiopeia

The constellation Cassiopeia ('The Queen') is near the North Star, so it is nearly always visible if you are in the Northern Hemisphere. Its five brightest stars also make a clear 'W' shape in the sky, making it easy to spot.

◄ Segin

**RUCHBAH**
This star is made up of two stars that are very close to one another and about 100 light years away from Earth.

► In ancient myth, Cassiopeia was the wife of King Cepheus of Ethiopia. She believed that she was even more beautiful than the goddesses.

Ruchbah ▲ (also called Ksora)

## SPOTTING CASSIOPEIA

If you live in the Northern Hemisphere, look towards the northeast soon after sunset on a clear autumn evening. You'll see five stars that make a wide 'W' shape, about one hand span across. If you live in the Southern Hemisphere, Cassiopeia appears low in the north at nightfall. It can also make an 'M' shape, depending on the time of night.

## Did you know ?

The names of many stars, such as Segin and Ruchbah, come from ancient Arabic words. From the 10th to the 15th centuries, the Arab world was at the centre of astronomical research.

## SPINNING STAR

In the middle of Cassiopeia's 'W' is Gamma Cassiopeia. It spins incredibly fast, throwing off material into the space around it. This makes it change in brightness throughout the year.

◀ Gamma Cassiopeia

Caph ▶

## CAPH AND SHEDIR

These giant stars are about twice the size of the Sun.

Shedir ▶

# Star-hopping to Perseus

Once you know the shape of Cassiopeia, you can use it to find the nearby constellation of Perseus ('The Hero'). Perseus follows Cassiopeia across the sky, night after night; it contains a couple of fantastic sights, so is really worth exploring.

▼ Perseus holds a
sword in one hand
and Medusa's head
in the other.

Mirphak ▼

◄ Mirphak is
the brightest
star in
Perseus. This
large star is
more than 60
times the size
of our Sun.

▲ Perseus

Medusa ▲

## PERSEUS AND MEDUSA
Perseus is a character from Greek mythology who killed an ugly monster called Medusa. She could turn people to stone by looking at them and she had snakes for her hair.

▲ Ruchbah

## HOPPING TO PERSEUS

Perseus is quite a faint constellation, so it's best to look for it on a clear and moonless night, when Cassiopeia is high in the sky. Draw an imaginary line from the middle star of Cassiopeia's 'W'– the star called Gamma Cassiopeia – above Ruchbah. Extend this line by about the width of Cassiopeia itself, and you'll reach an almost straight line of three stars, which make the arm and upper body of Perseus.

## Imagine this

At least four of the stars in Perseus have planets going around them. Imagine what the surface and weather might be like on these planets. Could there even be strange life-forms thriving on them?

Star clusters ▼

## CASSIOPEIA TO PERSEUS

On the way from Cassiopeia to Perseus, you'll pass a faint smudge. Look closely through a pair of binoculars and you may see that this is two star clusters, each containing hundreds of stars.

# The Summer Triangle

The Summer Triangle is not really a constellation but a pattern made up of three stars in three different constellations. The three stars – called Vega, Deneb and Altair – are all bright and high up in the sky in the summer months. Once you can find the stars, you can use the triangle to explore the night sky around them.

▲ Vega

Deneb ▶

## SPOTTING THE SUMMER TRIANGLE

It takes a little practice to pick out this triangle in the sky. In summer, face east in the late evening. Lie on your back and look up for three especially bright stars high in the sky. Start with the blue-white star Vega almost directly above you. Then look down towards the southern **horizon** to spot Altair, which is slightly less bright than Vega. The distance from Altair to Vega is about two hand spans. Then look northeast (to the left of Vega) to spot Deneb, the third star in the triangle.

## FINDING THE MILKY WAY

On a clear and moonless night, look between the stars Vega and Altair of the Summer Triangle. You may see a faint but broad band of light – this comes from the billions of stars in our own galaxy, the Milky Way. If you're lucky, you'll see a dark band across it. This is actually dust that blocks out the light in the background.

▼ Deneb

Vega ▼

◄ Altair

◄ Altair

## ASTROFACTS

>> Deneb is a supergiant star that has almost 80,000 times the luminous power of the Sun. Deneb is faint because it lies almost 1500 light-years from Earth.

>> Vega is 25 light-years away from Earth; nearly 1000 years ago it was the North Star, like Polaris is today.

>> Altair is just 17 light-years from Earth; it is one of the closest stars you can see at night.

# Star-hopping
## to Cygnus, Lyra and Aquila

This is a very simple starhop. Once you can see the Summer Triangle, you've already found the three constellations Cygnus ('The Swan'), Lyra ('The Lyre', a type of musical instrument) and Aquila ('The Eagle').

### CYGNUS

Stretching its wings over the Milky Way, it's easy to see why this constellation is called 'The Swan'. The tail of the swan is Deneb, one of the stars of the Summer Triangle, while its head is the star Albireo. This looks like a single star with the naked eye, but is actually two stars – a bright yellow one with a fainter blue partner.

◀ Vega

Albireo ▲

▲ Deneb

## LYRA

The star Vega from the Summer Triangle is the brightest star in Lyra. It is the fifth brightest star in the night sky. You can often see a parallelogram of four stars, which seems to be hanging from Vega.

## Imagine this

The constellation of Cygnus is home to a black hole nearly 15 times the mass of the Sun. It spins 800 times a second as it sucks in anything very close to it. Imagine what it would be like to fall into a black hole. You'd be stretched out like a piece of spaghetti!

▼ Tarazed

▲ Altair

## AQUILA

Altair, the third star of the Summer Triangle, is the brightest star in this constellation, which looks like an eagle in flight. If you have a pair of binoculars, take a close look around the star called Tarazed. You should see a strange E-shaped area of darkness, almost as big as the full Moon. This is a giant cloud of dust that blocks out the light from the stars behind.

## Did you know?

Although the Southern Cross was known by the ancient Greeks, it can no longer be seen from the country today. This is because Earth wobbles on its axis over thousands of years. This wobble has moved the Southern Cross out of sight.

▼ The two brightest stars of the Summer Cross make up the long arm of the cross. They are called Acrux and Gacrux.

▼ Acrux

Gacrux ▲

# The Southern Cross

If you live south of the equator, you'll nearly always be able to see the Southern Cross, or Crux, in the night sky. It is the smallest of all the 88 constellations, but is an important signpost to other stars. Ancient sailors used it to find their way around the seas.

# SPOTTING THE SOUTHERN CROSS

The Southern Cross is in the night sky over much of the Southern Hemisphere, and rarely dips below the horizon. During mid-summer, look towards the south and try to spot a cross or kite-like shape made up of four bright stars. This is the Southern Cross. It is very small – from top to bottom it measures only the width of four of your fingers held up close together at arms length.

▼ Coal Sack

◄ Right next to the Southern Cross, you may see a black patch on the background of the Milky Way. This is called the Coal Sack and it is a giant cloud of dust called a dark nebula.

New Zealand flag ▼

◄ Milky Way

The Southern Cross ► is so famous that it even appears on the national flags of Australia and New Zealand.

## CHECK OUT THE MILKY WAY

On a moonless night, away from bright city lights, look out for a band of stars stretching across the sky from south to north and passing through the Southern Cross. This band is the Milky Way. It appears as a slightly lighter band of sky and is packed with a huge number of stars.

# Star-hopping
## to Centaurus

The Southern Cross is a great starting point from which to explore other constellations in the Southern Hemisphere. From here you can easily find Centaurus ('The Centaur') – one of the largest and most interesting constellations in the sky.

Centaurus ▼

The constellation of ▶ Centaurus almost wraps around the Southern Cross.

Omega ▲ Centauri

## OLD FRIENDS

In the middle of the body of the Centaur is what looks like a smudged star. You can see it with your naked eye. This not a single star, but a cluster of more than one million stars called Omega Centauri. **Astronomers** think that it is more than 12 billion years old – one of the oldest things in our galaxy.

## HOPPING TO CENTAURUS

Start at the Southern Cross. Draw an imaginary line between the two stars in the short arm of the cross. Move along this line from the darker star in the arm to the brighter one, then carry on for three times this distance. You will arrive at a bright star called Beta Centauri. A little further along the imaginary line, you'll come to Alpha Centauri, the brightest star in this constellation.

▼ Centaurus is named after a type of creature in Greek myth called a centaur. Its body was half man, half horse.

Omega Centauri ▼

Beta Centauri

▼ Southern Cross

▲ Alpha Centauri

Look out for the phases of the inner planets, Mercury and Venus.

Find out what makes Mars the 'red planet' and what Saturn's rings are made of.

Learn about the orbits of the planets and how this affects what we can see from Earth.

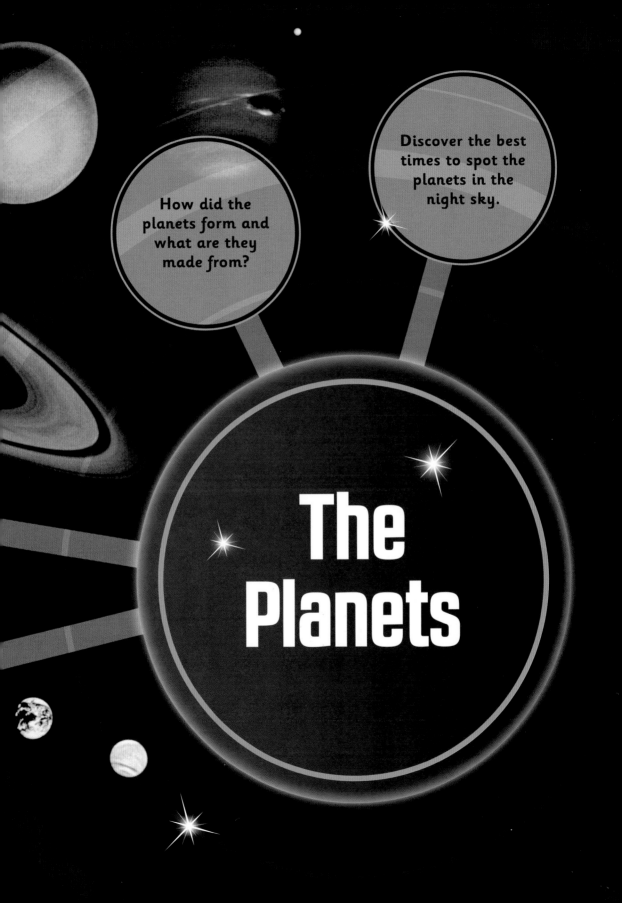

How did the planets form and what are they made from?

Discover the best times to spot the planets in the night sky.

# The Planets

# ASTROFACTS

>> The Sun and planets formed out of a giant cloud of gas and dust about 4.5 billion years ago.

>> Spacecraft have visited every planet in the Solar System, and we have landed probes on the surfaces of Venus, Mars, Saturn's moon Titan, some comets, asteroids and of course Earth's own Moon.

Mercury ▼

Earth ▼

◀ Sun

Venus ▲

Mars ▲

# The Solar System

With the Sun at its centre, our **Solar System** has eight planets –
including Earth – as well as more than 150 moons. Smaller
objects such as **asteroids** and comets are also part of the Solar
System, which is all held together by the giant Sun's **gravity**.

## ORBITING THE SUN

The **planets** and other objects in the Solar System orbit around
the Sun. Almost all follow a path roughly around the Sun's
equator. They orbit at very different speeds. The nearest planet to
the Sun, Mercury, moves at nearly 170,000 kilometres per hour,
while the furthest, Neptune, moves at 19,000 kilometres per hour.

▼ Jupiter

Uranus ▼

Neptune ▲

Saturn ▲

## SEEING THE PLANETS

Planets shine by reflecting light from the Sun. They do not make
their own light. The brightness of planets changes depending on
how far away they are from the Sun and how much of the sunlit
side is facing us. Venus and Jupiter can appear brighter than even
the brightest stars, such as Sirius and Vega.

# Planet watching

Five planets in our Solar System are bright enough to be seen without binoculars or a telescope. These are the three rocky planets, Mercury, Venus and Mars, and the two giant gas planets, Jupiter and Saturn. Large telescopes are required to get a good view of the other planets, Uranus and Neptune, as they are too far away.

## THE PATH OF THE PLANETS

The planets move from east to west across the sky. They all follow roughly the same path as the Moon and Sun. This means that sometimes the planets appear to be close together in the sky, or even line up.

▼ Jupiter

## Did you know?

The planets all move at different speeds and take different times to complete an orbit around the Sun. Saturn takes 30 years, Mercury just 88 days. The result is that they don't appear in the same patch of the sky from one year to the next.

## FINDING PLANETS

Because of their complex movements, the best way to find a planet in the sky is to check an astronomical magazine or website. This will tell you which constellation the planet passes through at any time of year. Find the constellation and look for an 'extra' star – this will be the planet!

▲ Mars in Leo

▼ Mars

◄ Venus

◄ Saturn

▲ On some nights, you can see several planets at the same time.

## THINGS TO DO

Get together with a group of friends and try acting out how the planets move around the Sun. In a garden or playground, mark out three large circles around the same centre. Place one person at the centre to be the Sun. Now three of you start walking around each of the three circles (orbits) to act as planets orbiting the Sun. Get the person in the inner circle to walk fastest and the person in the outer circle to walk slowest. Notice how the position of each person (or planet) changes compared to the others. That's why the movement of the planets, as seen from Earth, appears to be complicated.

# Venus

Venus is often mistaken for a UFO because it is the brightest object in the night sky after the Sun and Moon, and it seems to hover low over the horizon. On a dark, moonless night, the light from this planet can even cast a shadow here on Earth.

## THE GREENHOUSE PLANET

Venus is almost the same size as Earth, but orbits closer to the Sun than our planet does. Thick clouds cover Venus's surface and its atmosphere acts like a giant greenhouse, raising **temperatures** on Venus to around 480°C. That's hot enough to melt lead!

◄ Like a greenhouse, the atmosphere of Venus traps heat from the Sun. A long time ago, Venus may have been much cooler.

## MAKE A DATE

From the Northern Hemisphere good times to see Venus are:
- summer 2015 in the evenings
- autumn 2015 before dawn
- spring 2016 before dawn
- spring 2017 in the evenings
- autumn 2018 in the evenings
- spring 2019 before dawn
- autumn 2020 before dawn

# SPOTTING VENUS

It's not always possible to see Venus. Although it is bright, it is also low in the sky, so is often blocked by trees or buildings. The best times to look for Venus is either just before sunrise in the eastern sky, or after sunset in the west.

Venus ▶

Moon ▶

## ASTROFACTS

>> Venus is about 108 million kilometres from the Sun and around 12,100 kilometres across.

>> The planet's atmosphere is mostly carbon dioxide.

>> Gravity on Venus is almost as strong as on Earth.

This picture of ▲ Venus was taken by a spacecraft called Pioneer in 1979.

# The phases of Venus

The brightness and size of Venus seems to change over time. This is because its orbit brings it closer to us and also takes it further away. As it moves around the Sun, Venus goes through **phases** when seen from Earth, just like the Moon does.

## THE CHANGING FACE OF VENUS

Like the Moon, Venus changes from a full disc, to a half disc, to a crescent in the sky. This cycle takes almost 580 days. When Venus journeys away from the Sun towards Earth, it can be seen in the early evening sky. As it starts to move away from Earth, it is visible in the early morning sky.

When Venus is on the other side of the Sun from Earth, it looks 'full' but smaller.

Venus ▶

Sun ▶

The best times to see Venus are when it is half lit by the Sun. It is bright and close enough to look big.

When Venus is closest to Earth, it seems bigger, but appears only as a thin crescent.

Earth ▶

Venus's surface can be ▶
seen in this picture
made by bouncing radar
off the planet.

## THE SURFACE OF VENUS

Although Venus is covered in thick cloud, space probes have given us fantastic images of its rocky surface. The planet has many of the same features that we have on Earth – such as **volcanoes**, mountains, plains and craters.

▲ Valleys on Venus can be up to 100 kilometres in length.

## PROBING THE PLANET

Many spacecraft have been sent to Venus to probe its atmosphere and surface. Some have even landed on the planet. In 1982, a Soviet spacecraft called Venera 13, was the first to send back colour photographs of the surface of Venus. The probe lasted only a few hours on Venus's hot surface.

▲ Scientists assemble the Venera 13 probe.

# Mercury

Mercury is the closest planet to the Sun and takes just 88 days to complete a full orbit – which means that a year on Mercury is only 88 days long! Mercury is barely larger than our Moon, and even looks a lot like the Moon, with lots of craters on its surface.

## SPOTTING MERCURY

Mercury is the smallest planet in the Solar System and very faint in our sky. It is difficult to spot without a good pair of binoculars. You can sometimes catch it as a tiny speck of light about half an hour before the Sun rises or after sunset. You will never see Mercury in the middle of the night.

A crater on the surface ▶
of Mercury.

### NORTH AND SOUTH

It's hard to wake up before dawn to see Mercury, so the best time to look is in the evening, just after sunset. If you live in the Northern Hemisphere, look out for Mercury low in the sky towards the west after sunset between April and June. If you're in the Southern Hemisphere try to spot it between September and November.

## MISSION TO MERCURY

Since 2008, NASA's spacecraft called Messenger has been orbiting around Mercury, beaming back sharp images and data about the planet. Scientists are trying to understand more about how the planet formed and why it has water ice in its dark craters.

Mercury orbits closer to the Sun than the Earth. To see the tiny planet, you need to look towards the Sun after sunset or before sunrise.

▲ Special shields are used to protect Messenger from high temperatures so close to the Sun.

Jupiter ▼

▲ Mercury

## Did you know?

The planet Mercury was named after the Roman messenger god because it goes around the Sun so quickly. The ancient myth showed the messenger with both a winged hat and winged sandals that helped him fly swiftly.

◀ Roman God Mercury

# Mercury's icy poles

Despite being close to the Sun, Mercury has ice in the craters near its poles. That's because sunlight never reaches into the depths of the craters, which remain at low temperatures.

▼ This picture, taken by NASA's Mariner 10 spacecraft shows the scars on the planet's surface caused by impacts with asteroids.

## PHASES OF MERCURY

Just like Venus and the Moon, Mercury has phases. It changes from full, to half, to a crescent, though you need a telescope to see these changes.

## ASTROFACTS

>> Mercury is 58 million kilometres away from the Sun.

>> The planet is only slightly larger than Earth's Moon.

>> The temperature on Mercury's surface is around 450°C during daytime and drops to -210°C or lower at night.

▼ Mercury orbits closer to the Sun than does our planet. Every few years it can be seen as a tiny black disc slowly moving in front of the Sun. This event is called a transit.

▲ A transit of Mercury across the Sun.

◄ Mercury's gravity is only about one third as strong as Earth's – not strong enough to hold on to any atmosphere.

# Mars

The planet Mars is our neighbour in space. It is often called the red planet because its surface is made up of rocks that are rich in iron oxide (rust). When seen with the naked eye, Mars looks like a bright star with a reddish colour.

## SPOTTING MARS

Mars is only half the diameter of Earth. Most of the time it looks like a reddish star in the sky. One way to tell it apart from stars is that Mars does not twinkle in the sky, while stars do.

Mars' orbit

Earth's orbit

Sun ▶

Earth ▶

◀ Opposition

## CLOSE ENCOUNTERS

Once every two years and two months, the orbits of Mars and Earth bring them close together and Mars appears very bright. This is what astronomers call 'opposition'. At these times, Mars can be seen rising in the east in the evening, soon after sunset.

## Imagine this

Billions of years ago, there were rivers of water on the surface of Mars and maybe even an ocean. But the temperature on Mars became too low and its atmosphere too thin, and there is no liquid water there today.

## LOOK OUT FOR MARS AT ITS BRIGHTEST

Mars will be in opposition at these times. It will appear bright red and shine more than twice as brightly as the brightest star.

- April to June 2016
- July to September 2018
- October to December 2020

Mars, god ▶ of war

◀ Mars seen ▶ in opposition.

## THE GOD OF WAR

Mars is named after the Roman god of war, because of its blood-red colour.

# The Martian surface

Mars is the only planet whose surface can be seen from Earth. With a good telescope you can see the bright ice caps on the planet's poles and a large dark area on its surface. But Mars also has vast extinct volcanoes and a huge canyon that splits the planet across the middle.

## ASTROFACTS

>> Mars orbits at an average distance of 228 million kilometres from the Sun.

>> The planet is 6794 kilometres across and its atmosphere is mostly carbon dioxide.

>> The temperature on Mars's surface is -75°C or lower at night and -2°C in the daytime.

>> Mars has two small moons called Phobos and Deimos.

### COULD I LIVE THERE?

Mars is a very unfriendly planet. You can't breathe in its carbon dioxide atmosphere and there is no liquid water on its surface today. If you stepped outside your shelter without a spacesuit, your body would explode because the Martian atmosphere is so thin!

Ice cap ▶

A picture of ▶
Mars taken by
the Mars
Surveyor
spacecraft.

Dark areas of dust ▶

Ice clouds ▶

Deep canyons ▶

## MARTIAN CANALS

In the 19th century, astronomers looked at Mars through their telescopes and drew patterns they saw on its surface. They believed that Mars was criss-crossed by canals built by Martians. Using powerful telescopes and spacecraft, we now know that the canals were made by water beds and rivers that flowed there billions of years ago.

The 'canals' on Mars, drawn by ▶
19th-century astronomers.

## MISSIONS TO MARS

Mars has been explored by a series of spacecraft. The first probes landed on Mars in 1976. They were called Viking 1 and 2 and took amazing photos of the red planet. More recently, scientists have sent wheeled vehicles to Mars to explore its surface, monitor its dust storms and seasons, and test its soil for traces of life.

# Jupiter

Jupiter is the largest planet in the Solar System – so big that all the other planets could easily fit inside it! Jupiter appears white in the sky and shines brighter than the brightest star Sirius, making it easy to spot.

## SPOTTING JUPITER

Jupiter is so bright that it can even cast a faint shadow on a very dark night. It takes Jupiter almost 12 years to orbit the Sun. This means it moves slowly in our skies and can be visible in one constellation for many months. One of the best times to view Jupiter is when it is directly opposite the Sun, with Earth in between. At these times, Jupiter appears at its highest point in the sky around midnight wherever you live.

Earth ▶

Jupiter ▶

### MAKE A DATE
To catch Jupiter at its brightest, look for it at the following times:
- February 2015 around the constellation of Cancer
- March 2016 around Leo
- April 2017 around Virgo
- May 2018 around Libra
- June 2019 around Ophiuchus

>> Jupiter orbits the Sun at an average distance of 778 million kilometres.

>> The planet is 142,800 kilometres across.

>> The temperature at the tops of Jupiter's clouds is -110°C.

## A GAS GIANT

Jupiter is a giant planet mostly made of hydrogen and helium gas, with no solid surface to stand on. It is surrounded by a very faint set of rings made of dark dust. There are at least 67 moons going around Jupiter, four of which are very large.

# The giant planet

Jupiter's great size means that its gravity is two and a half times that on Earth. This big pull has trapped many moons and a system of dusty rings that now orbit the planet.

## JUPITER'S MOONS

Try spotting Jupiter's moons. Look at the planet through a pair of good binoculars — you'll need to hold them very steady. You should notice up to four little dots in a straight line either side of Jupiter. The dots are Jupiter's four largest moons called Ganymede, Io, Europa and Callisto. The moons orbit quickly around the giant planet. If you watch them over many nights, you will see that they change position around Jupiter.

▼ Jupiter

Moons ▲

## Did you know ?

Jupiter has a swirling atmosphere. A giant storm on Jupiter, called the Great Red Spot, has been blowing there for more than 300 years! This storm is so big that two Earths could fit inside it. The winds blow at speeds of around 600 kilometres per hour.

Great Red Spot ▼

## GALILEO

The moons of Jupiter were discovered in 1610 by the Italian scientist Galileo Galilei using an early telescope. His study was important because it suggested that Earth orbited the Sun – and not the other way round as many people believed at the time. Galileo's name was used by NASA for the spacecraft it sent to investigate Jupiter in 2003.

Galileo Galilei ▶

▲ Galileo spacecraft

◀ Comet impact

▼ Dark collision spots

## COMET CRASH

Jupiter's huge gravitational pull trapped a passing comet and pulled it to pieces. In 1994, pieces of the comet – called Shoemaker-Levy 9 – plummeted into the planet's cloudy atmosphere and left behind dark spots.

# Saturn

Saturn is the sixth planet from the Sun and the second largest of the eight planets in the Solar System. The distant planet appears pale yellow in the sky, always dimmer than Jupiter or Venus, but it still outshines almost all of the stars at night.

Inside Saturn's ▼ rings.

## LORD OF THE RINGS

Like Jupiter, Saturn is a giant gas planet. Beneath clouds of hydrogen and helium gas, the interior gradually becomes a giant ball of liquid. Saturn is famous for the beautiful rings around its centre, which are made of millions of rocks and lots of dust, all covered in ice.

## Imagine this

Saturn is made mostly of hydrogen and helium, the lightest of all the chemical elements. So even though it is nearly ten times the diameter of our planet, its gravity is only just stronger than Earth's.

# SPOTTING SATURN

Saturn takes a long time to complete one orbit of the Sun – its year is more than 29 Earth years long! This means that Saturn appears to move very slowly across the background of constellations in the sky. It takes around two years to cross one constellation, which makes it fairly easy to see in the sky. It looks like a bright, golden star.

**MAKE A DATE**

To find Saturn, look for the constellation that it is passing through:
- Between 2014 and 2015 Saturn will be in the constellation of Libra
- From 2016 to 2018 it will be in Ophiuchus
- From 2019 to 2020 the planet will be in Sagittarius

Saturn in Taurus ▲

# Rings and moons

Saturn's amazing rings probably formed when asteroids and comets got too close to the planet and were torn apart by its gravity. The rings are around 250,000 kilometres across, but only 1.5 kilometres thick. Trying to spot the rings is a challenge, but worth a try for an exciting sight.

## SPOTTING THE RINGS

You'll need a small telescope to see Saturn's rings. Choose a dark, clear night and look closely at Saturn; the rings will look like handles sticking out from either side of the planet.

Telescopic view ▲ of Saturn.

## AT FULL TILT

When seen from Earth, Saturn's rings change their tilt towards us from year to year. Sometimes the rings are edge-on, and because they are very thin, we can't see them at all. Between 2014 to 2020 the rings will be more open and facing us, making it a good time to look. The rings will be fully displayed in 2017, and Saturn will appear very bright.

◄ Saturn's rings tilt in and out of view every few years.

▼ Saturn's north polar cyclone.

## POLAR CYCLONES

NASA's Cassini spacecraft reached Saturn in 2004 and sent back some fantastic images of the planet. At the poles of the planet are huge cyclones – 20 times as big as those on Earth. Heat from the interior of Saturn powers these giant thunderstorms.

▼ An artist's impression of Titan.

## Did you know?

Saturn has 62 moons. The largest, called Titan, has an atmosphere. Scientists landed a spacecraft called Huygens on Titan in January 2005. The spacecraft sent back images to Earth showing that Titan is a strange place with lakes and rivers of oil!

The Moon is the biggest and brightest object in the night sky – discover how and when it formed.

The Moon seems to change shape over a month – learn how to predict its phases and understand why they happen.

Why can we only see one side of the Moon? Find out about the Moon's dark side.

# The Moon

Observe the surface of the Moon and identify its craters and seas.

Find out where missions to the Moon have landed.

# Moon watching

No matter where you live, the Moon is a wonderful object to explore at night. Unlike the stars, the Moon does not make its own light. The Moon shines because it reflects the light from the Sun. Since the Moon is much closer to us than the stars or planets, it is the brightest and biggest object in the night sky.

## Did you know?

The Moon formed around 4.5 billion years ago when a rock as big as Mars smashed into Earth. Chunks of material broke off and went into orbit around our planet. Slowly, these rocks stuck together to become our Moon.

## THE DARK SIDE OF THE MOON

From Earth, we can see only one side of the Moon. This is because the Moon spins at the same rate as it orbits the Earth, constantly turning one face away from us. This is sometimes called the 'dark side' of the Moon and it can only be seen from a spacecraft.

# SPOTTING THE MOON

When the Moon is in the sky, you won't have any trouble spotting it with your naked eye. Even a small pair of binoculars will reveal lots of detail on its surface.

## ASTROFACTS

>> The Moon is about 380,000 kilometres away from Earth.

>> If Earth were the size of a basketball, the Moon would be the size of a tennis ball.

>> The Moon has no atmosphere. The temperature on its surface can fall as low as -150°C.

▲ Crescent Moon    ▲ Half Moon    ▲ Three-quarter Moon

# The Moon's phases

We know that the Moon is ball-shaped, so why does it sometimes look like a circle and sometimes a crescent? Of course the Moon itself doesn't change shape; what changes is how much of the sunlit part of the Moon that we can see as it orbits Earth. The different shapes of the Moon are called its phases.

## Did you know?

The phases of the Moon are very important to life on Earth. The tides in the Earth's seas, the behaviour of animals and even the dates of religious festivals are affected by the position of the Moon.

The date on which Easter ▶ Sunday falls is set by the phases of the Moon.

▼ Full Moon

Three-quarter Moon ▲  Half Moon ▲  Crescent Moon ▲

## OUR VIEW OF THE MOON
From Earth, the phases of the Moon can be seen clearly. When the Moon is getting bigger in the sky, it is called a waxing Moon; when it is getting smaller, it is called a waning Moon.

# THINGS TO DO

Every night for one month, look at the Moon. Make one drawing of the Moon's shape each night. Label your sketch with the date, time and what phase you think it is.

Saturday
23 March
9.20pm

Crescent
Moon

# The Moon's surface

You can explore the Moon's craters, highlands and seas. Different features are visible as the Moon changes phase.

## SPOTTING CRATERS

Look for craters when the Moon is bigger than a half circle. They were made when meteors or asteroids hit the surface.

## ARISTARCHUS

On the upper left of the Moon, this crater is one of the brightest spots you can see. It is 450 million years old.

## COPERNICUS

Below and to the right of Aristarchus, this crater is more than one kilometre deep. It is named after the Polish astronomer Nicolaus Copernicus.

## TYCHO

This crater is towards the bottom of the Moon. It is 85 kilometres across. The bright rays coming out from it were made when a giant meteor struck the Moon.

## THE MOON'S SEAS

The dark patches on the Moon are called seas, but they don't hold any water. Instead, they are smooth, rocky plains, made when molten rock flooded parts of the Moon's surface long ago.

## ASTROFACTS

>> The gravity on the surface of the Moon is six times weaker than on Earth.

>> The tallest mountain on the Moon is Mons Huygens – it is almost half as tall as Mount Everest.

>> There are no active volcanoes on the Moon.

## LOOK OUT FOR THE TERMINATOR

The **terminator** is the dividing line between the sunlit part of the Moon and the part that is in darkness.

Terminator ▶

# Exploring the Moon

The Moon is the only place in our Solar System – apart from Earth – where people have walked. Six manned spacecraft and many more robot probes have landed on the Moon. They sent back lots of information and even collected rock samples from the surface.

## LOOKING FOR APOLLO

Using a pair of binoculars, try to find the places where the six Apollo spacecraft landed on the Moon. Use the picture of the Moon here to help you. The locations of the Moon's craters and dark seas make great pointers.

This crater, called Kepler, is a smaller version of the brighter crater Copernicus.

This dark patch is called the Sea of Serenity; it is about 600 kilometres across.

Apollo 15

Apollo 17

The dark Sea of Crisis is easily visible with the naked eye. It is 550 kilometres wide.

▲ Landing module

Apollo 12

The Sea of Moisture can be seen with the naked eye. It is about 350 kilometres wide.

The Sea of Tranquillity is a smooth plain; it was the site of the very first Moon walk.

Apollo 16

Apollo 14

Apollo 11

## THE FIRST VISIT

The first spacecraft to land safely on the Moon was launched by the Soviet Union in 1966. This robot probe was called Luna 9. It took pictures of the Moon's surface and measured levels of radiation.

▲ Luna 9 probe

## MANNED MISSIONS

Only six manned spacecraft have landed on the Moon. These were all part of NASA's Apollo programme. The first, Apollo 11, landed on 20 July 1969 on the fairly flat surface of the Sea of Tranquillity. The last mission, Apollo 17, was in 1972.

▲ **Astronaut** Neil Armstrong was the first person to walk on the Moon.

# Lunar eclipses

A lunar eclipse is a rare but beautiful sight in the night sky. It happens when the Moon passes through the shadow cast by Earth. For this to occur, the full Moon and Sun must be exactly on opposite sides of Earth. This does not happen often, and so lunar eclipses can only be seen on Earth about twice a year.

## WATCHING LUNAR ECLIPSES

You can enjoy watching a total lunar eclipse with unaided eyes or binoculars. A lunar eclipse takes several hours from start to finish, with the Moon completely covered by Earth's shadow for about one hour. Since the eclipse occurs slowly, a good way to watch it is to look at the Moon every 20 minutes and keep track of how the shadowed part of the Moon is changing.

The shadow of Earth ▲ passes over the Moon during an eclipse.

## HOW ECLIPSES HAPPEN

Earth's shadow passes slowly over the Moon during an eclipse. Sometimes the Moon is completely shadowed by Earth; this is called a total eclipse. Sometimes the Moon only passes through the edge of Earth's shadow; this is called a partial eclipse.

Sun ▶

## TURNING RED!

When the Moon goes into the shadow of Earth during a total eclipse, it turns an orange colour. This is because light from the Sun bends slightly as it passes through Earth's atmosphere. Dust in the atmosphere turns the light orange before it strikes the Moon.

### MAKE A DATE

Total lunar eclipses will occur on these dates at these places:

- 8 October 2014: Australia, South America
- 4 April 2015: Asia, Australia, South America
- 27 July 2018: Europe, Africa, Asia, Australia
- 21 January 2019: Europe, Africa, South America

Moon's orbit ········>

Full shadow

Earth ▶

Moon ▶

Sun's rays

Faint shadow

Solar eclipses are awesome sights. See how they happen and find out when the next one is due, and how to watch it safely.

Meteor showers can light up the sky – but where and when can you see them?

What is a comet and when can you expect to see one? Learn more about these spectacular balls of dirty ice.

# Unusual Sights

Discover how the solar wind causes our atmosphere to light up.

Find out the difference between a meteor and a meteorite.

# Meteors

Meteors are nature's fireworks. These quick-moving streaks of light in the night sky are sometimes called 'shooting stars', but they having nothing at all to do with stars. Rather, they are small rocky objects or particles from space that burn up when they enter Earth's atmosphere.

## METEOR SHOWERS

You can see meteors at any time of the year, but some months are especially good for seeing lots of these 'shooting stars'. Meteor showers can be spectacular, with hundreds of meteors visible in an hour, all seeming to come from one part of the night sky.

## GETTING PREPARED

You don't need any equipment to watch meteor showers – just your eyes! For the best chance of seeing a meteor shower, check when a shower is due, and look in the area of its constellation. If possible, choose a dark, moonless night and move well away from street lights.

Lie back on the ground or on a ▲ deckchair and watch the show.

Earth

Comet

Comet
dust

## BURNING COMET DUST

Comets that pass close to Earth leave behind huge amounts of tiny dust particles. Meteor showers occur when Earth – in its orbit around the Sun – passes through those leftover bits of comet dust. When this happens, lots of dust grains crash into Earth's atmosphere and burn up to make a meteor shower.

Did you know?

A meteor is a particle – from a dust grain to a small rock in size – that burns up in Earth's atmosphere. If it does not completely burn up and crashes to the ground, it is then known as a meteorite.

◄ Meteorite

Meteor streaks ▲

▲ Look for the
shape of Perseus
in the sky.

▲ Meteor streaks

# The Perseids shower

The Perseids meteor shower happens every year between July and August. At the peak of the shower in mid-August, there can be between 50 and 75 streaks every hour. However, if you are watching from the Southern Hemisphere you might only see about 10 to 20 meteors per hour.

## ASTROFACTS

>> The dust that makes the Perseids meteor shower was left behind by a comet called Swift-Tuttle.

>> Comet Swift-Tuttle was last seen in our skies in 1992 and won't appear again until 2126.

>> The meteors that burn up in Earth's atmosphere move at nearly 215,000 kilometres per hour.

# SPOTTING THE PERSEIDS

The Perseids shower appears to spread out from the constellation of Perseus. Look up at that area of the sky, and at patches of dark sky around this constellation.

▲ If you like camping, why not plan a trip that coincides with the dates of the meteor showers.

# The Leonids shower

The Leonids meteor shower is special because it can turn into a meteor storm. In 1966, night sky watchers in the United States of America saw nearly 3000 meteors every minute! But the big storms are rare and most years you will normally see about 10 to 20 meteors every hour.

## SPOTTING THE LEONIDS

The best time of the year to look out for the Leonid meteors is from mid to late November. The shower is clearer after midnight and it helps if it's a moonless night. The meteors appear in all parts of the sky, but if you trace them back, you'll see that they spread out from the constellation of Leo. The Leonids can be seen from both hemispheres.

### METEOR STORM

People watching the Leonids in 1833 said they could see 100,000 meteors in the sky every hour. Some made drawings of this amazing sight. The next big Leonids storm is due in 2023, when Earth will pass through a thick cloud of comet dust.

The Leonids meteor ▲ shower of 1833.

From 2014 to 2020 look out for the Leonids between the nights of 16 and 18 November.

## ASTROFACTS

>> The Leonids meteor shower is caused by Earth passing through the dust left behind by a comet called Tempel-Tuttle.

>> The light streaks you see are particles burning up in Earth's atmosphere with temperatures as high as 1650°C. Most of the particles are no bigger than peas.

# The Geminids shower

The Geminds meteor shower is one of the best of the year. You can see it from both hemispheres, over all parts of the world. This shower gets its name from the constellation of Gemini, because the meteors seem to spread out from that part of the sky.

▼ Look out for the constellation of Gemini ('The Twins').

## FIREBALLS
In the Southern Hemisphere, the constellation of Gemini is always close to the horizon, so you're likely to see fewer meteors than in the Northern Hemisphere. If you get lucky, the Geminids shower can produce a few very bright 'fireballs' that really light up the night sky!

# SPOTTING THE GEMINIDS

You can see the Geminids meteor shower every year during the first three weeks of December. It's at its most spectacular around 14–15 December. The best time to look is from 9pm onwards when you may see up to 120 meteor flashes every hour.

# THINGS TO DO

After you've watched a meteor shower, try drawing what you saw. Take a large piece of black paper and use white, yellow and orange chalk to draw the streaks of light in the sky. Show the horizon and any tall trees and buildings too. Try to add in the constellation from which the meteors seemed to spread out.

▲ A Geminid meteor fireball.

# Dancing lights in the sky

Sometimes the night sky shimmers with a beautiful display of glowing lights called **aurorae**. You can usually see aurorae only in countries that are close to Earth's North or South poles, such as Iceland, Norway, Canada, Southern Australia and New Zealand.

## SPOTTING AURORAE

Watching aurorae is very simple, but you need a clear, dark night and lots of electric action in the atmosphere. Try to find a spot in the countryside, away from city lights. Around midnight, let your eyes get used to the dark then face north (or south if you are in the Southern Hemisphere), and look close to the horizon. The aurorae mostly appear as faint green or reddish glows.

### WHAT ARE AURORAE?

Aurorae happen because super-hot gases are thrown off by the Sun. These gases include electrified particles. When they reach Earth's magnetic field, they get dragged into Earth's atmosphere near the North and South poles. They smash into **atoms** in the atmosphere, making glowing halos of light.

Aurorae are named after the Roman goddess of dawn – Aurora – who brought the light of day in her chariot. In the Northern Hemisphere these dancing light shows are called the *aurora borealis*, or Northern Lights. In the Southern Hemisphere, they are called the *aurora australis*, or Southern Lights.

Roman goddess ▲
Aurora

# ASTROFACTS

>> Most aurorae occur about 100 kilometres up in the atmosphere.

>> The particles thrown out by the Sun take at least two days to travel the 150 million kilometres to Earth.

>> Aurorae can be green, yellow, orange or red, and look like rippling sheets of light.

International ▲
Space Station

# Fleeting satellites

**Right now, there are around 2500 artificial satellites and spacecraft orbiting Earth. Many of the satellites can be seen in the night sky because, like the planets and the Moon, they reflect sunlight.**

## EYES IN THE SKY

Satellites are vital to modern life. They send telephone and television signals around the world, help to predict the weather and gather important information about our planet and the Universe beyond. To stay in orbit, satellites zoom around Earth at nearly 30,000 kilometres per hour, and complete a lap around the planet in just two hours.

# SPOTTING SATELLITES

On a dark night you can spot more than 20 satellites passing across the sky every hour. You'll need to have a good view over a wide region of the night sky. Unlike meteors, which streak by in a flash, a satellite will appear as a star-like speck of light that lingers for five minutes or more as it travels from one horizon to the other. Most satellites travel from west to east.

## INTERNATIONAL SPACE STATION

The International Space Station (ISS) is the largest object we have ever built in space. It is about the size of a football field. The ISS orbits about 360 kilometres above Earth and sometimes appears brighter than Venus! The ISS can be seen just before sunrise or after sunset, crossing the sky from the west. It might look like a fast-moving aeroplane, but the ISS does not have any flashing lights.

The International Space ▲
Station passes overhead at a
speed of 27,000 km/h.

## ASTROFACTS

>> Most satellites orbit about 400 kilometres above our planet.

>> The first man-made object orbited Earth in 1957. It was a basketball-sized satellite called Sputnik 1.

Sputnik 1 ▲

# Solar eclipses

A solar eclipse may be the greatest show in the sky. It happens when the Moon passes directly between the Sun and Earth. The Moon then blocks out most of the Sun's light. A total eclipse of the Sun only happens about once every two years.

## HOW ECLIPSES HAPPEN

Solar eclipses are rare because the Sun, Moon and Earth have to be in exactly the right places in space. And you have to be standing in the right place on Earth, at the right time, to see it! Sometimes the Moon only covers a part of the Sun, allowing sunlight to still get through. This is called a partial eclipse.

▲ Partial eclipse

## BITING THE SUN

When an eclipse starts, you'll see the Moon move slowly across the Sun. It looks like the Moon has taken a bite out of the Sun! Slowly over the next few hours the 'bite' will get larger and larger. Finally the Moon will fully cover the Sun. This moment is called **totality**, and lasts only a few minutes. The light of day turns into dark night! You might notice a few stars, birds will stop singing and it may feel slightly cooler.

Sun ▶

Sun's rays

The stages of ▶ an eclipse

## DANGER! WARNING!

You must NEVER look directly at the Sun with your eyes, or through binoculars or a telescope. Looking at the Sun is very dangerous and can cause blindness. To find out how to watch an eclipse safely, turn to the next page.

turn to the next page.

# ASTROFACTS

>> During a solar eclipse the Moon's shadow moves across the surface of Earth at more than 1500 kilometres per hour.

>> Total solar eclipses happen about once every 1.5 years.

>> There are at least two partial eclipses per year somewhere on Earth.

A total eclipse is ▼ visible only where the Moon passes right in front of the Sun.

Total eclipse visible

Night-time

Earth ◄

Moon ▲

Partial eclipse visible

Moon's orbit

# Watching eclipses safely

To watch a solar eclipse, get the help of an adult. You can't look directly at the Sun so you'll need to project its image onto a screen by making a simple pinhole viewer (see right).

## WATCHING THROUGH GLASSES

You can buy special eclipse glasses that safely filter most of the Sun's rays. Wearing these glasses can let you watch a solar eclipse safely for a few minutes. Ask an adult to buy a pair of these glasses – they are NOT the same as sunglasses!

In a total eclipse, ▲ you may see the ghostly white light of the Sun's outermost region, called the corona, as it shimmers around the Moon.

Solar eclipse glasses ▲

# THINGS TO DO

❶ To make a pinhole viewer, you'll need two pieces of stiff card, one of which must be white because it will be your 'screen'. Cut a small square into one card, and then tape a piece of aluminium foil over the square.

❷ Next make a pinhole in the middle of the foil.

❸ Place the other white card (screen) on the ground or against a chair. With the Sun behind you, hold up the card with the pinhole and line it up so that the Sun's image falls on the white card. You'll have to move the pinhole card back and forth to get a sharp and large image of the Sun on the white card.

## MAKE A DATE

Total solar eclipses will be visible on these dates at these places:
- 20 March 2015: parts of Iceland, Europe, North America and Asia
- 9 March 2016: East Asia and Australia
- 21 August 2017: parts of North and South America
- 2 July 2019: South America
- 14 December 2020: South America

Bright comets often ▶ show two flowing tails, making a 'V' shape. One of the tails is blue and made of gas. The other is creamy yellow and made of dust.

# Great comets

A bright comet with a huge tail sweeping across the night sky is one of nature's most amazing sights. Comets don't appear often, but when they do, be prepared and make the most of it. Some comets only get close enough to be seen once every 200 years!

## WHAT ARE COMETS?

Comets are big dusty snowballs that travel round the Sun in very long, stretched-out orbits. They are icy leftovers from the time that the Sun and Solar System formed about 4.5 billion years ago. The icy part of a comet, called its nucleus, is quite small – few are much more than 15 kilometres across.

▲ The nucleus of the comet called Tempel 1.

110

## THE TAIL OF A COMET

Most of the time, comets are so far from the Sun that we cannot see them. But when the long orbit of a comet brings it close to the Sun, something special happens. The heat of the Sun warms the ice of the comet's nucleus and boils it off. The boiled ice and dust forms tails that stream millions of kilometres behind the comet, always pointing away from the Sun. We can then see the comet as a glowing head with a long tail.

## THE PATH OF A COMET

A comet's elongated orbit brings it close to the Sun. This is when the comet becomes visible.

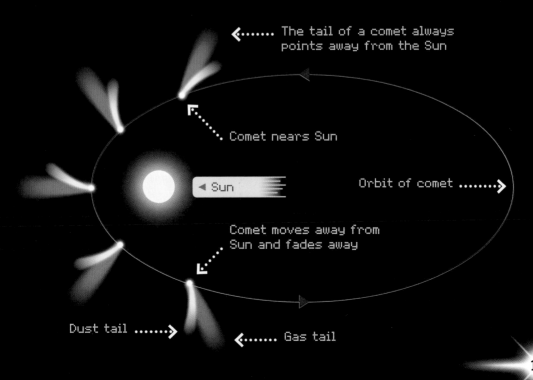

The tail of a comet always points away from the Sun

Comet nears Sun

◄ Sun

Orbit of comet ........►

Comet moves away from Sun and fades away

Dust tail ......►

◄...... Gas tail

## ASTROFACTS

>> Comet Halley is one of the best-known comets. It last appeared in our skies in 1986, but won't return again until 2061.

>> In July 1994 a comet called Shoemaker-Levy 9 broke apart and smashed into the giant planet Jupiter.

>> Some comets crash into the Sun and vanish.

# Spotting comets

Some comets appear in our skies regularly every few hundred years. But others are less predictable. Even astronomers can't be sure when the next great comet will come. The biggest comets can easily be seen, even from brightly lit towns and cities.

## GREAT COMETS OF THE PAST

There have been some amazing comets in history. The great comet of 1744 was so bright that it be could be seen in the morning sky. Comet Ikeya-Seki was the brightest of the 20th century. In October 1965 it was nearly ten times brighter than the full Moon!

▲ This painting shows Donati's Comet over London in 1858.

## Did you know?

Comets are such an awesome sight in the sky that people in the past thought they were messages from the gods. Because some comets looked like swords in the sky, some people took them to be signs of war and disaster to come.

## WHERE TO LOOK

When a comet appears, it doesn't move across the sky in a flash, like a meteor. Because comets are very far away, they stay in the sky from night to night, for weeks. Most comets are faint and you'll need binoculars to see them. Even then, you may only see the tail. You'll need to check astronomical websites to find out where to look.

# Glossary

## ASTEROID
A large rocky object in the Solar System. Most asteroids orbit the Sun in a belt between Mars and Jupiter.

## ASTRONAUT
A person who travels in space.

## ASTRONOMER
A scientist who studies objects in space, such as planets and stars.

## ATMOSPHERE
Layers of gases that surround a planet, moon or star.

## ATOM
A miniscule building block that makes up all matter.

## AURORAE
Light displays caused by particles from the Sun that enter the Earth's (or other planet's) atmosphere around the north or south poles.

## BILLION
The number equal to a 1000 million. It is written as 1 followed by 9 zeros.

## BLACK HOLE
A region of space around a very small and extremely massive object within which the gravity is so strong that not even light can escape.

## CARBON DIOXIDE
A gas given off by animals and taken in by plants. It is present in the atmospheres of several planets.

## COMET
A small icy object made of gas and dust, which orbits around the Sun.

## CONSTELLATION
An imaginary pattern or shape drawn in the sky by connecting lines between different stars.

## DAY
The length of time it takes Earth (or any planet) to spin once on its axis.

## DIAMETER
The length of a straight line passing through the centre of a circle and connecting two points on the circumference (the edge of the circle).

## DUST (IN SPACE)
Tiny solid particles that float in the space between stars.

## ECLIPSE
The event that occurs when one body in space passes in front of another and blocks out the light from the more distant of the two objects.

## ELEMENT
A pure chemical, such as hydrogen, oxygen, carbon, iron and so on.

## EQUATOR (EARTH'S)
The line around the Earth that is the boundary between the Northern and Southern Hemispheres.

## GALAXY
A collection of billions of stars, gas and dust held together by gravity.

## GRAVITY
A force that pulls two objects together. It depends on the amount of matter in the objects and their distance apart.

## HELIUM
The second lightest and second most common element in the Universe. The product of the nuclear fusion of hydrogen in stars.

## HEMISPHERE
The half of Earth (or planet) between the North or South Pole and the equator.

## HORIZON
The line where the ground and sky appear to meet.

## HYDROGEN
The lightest and most common element in the Universe.

## LATITUDE
The location of a point on Earth relative to the equator. There are ninety degrees of latitude north and south of the line of the equator.

## LIGHT-YEAR
The distance travelled by light in space in one year. This is a distance of 9,500,000,000,000 kilometres.

## LONGITUDE
The location of a point on Earth relative to an imaginary line that passes from north to south through Greenwich, England. It is measured in degrees east or west of that line.

## MATTER
Substance that occupies space and has mass.

## METEOR
A bright streak of light in the sky caused when a small rocky object enters Earth's atmosphere and burns up.

## METEORITE
The remains of a rocky and metallic object that plunges from space to Earth's surface.

## MILKY WAY
A spiral galaxy that contains over 100 billion stars, including the Sun and its Solar System.

## MILLION
The number 1,000,000, written as 1 followed by 6 zeros.

## MOON
A small rocky body that moves around a planet.

## NEBULA
A cloud of gas and dust in space. New stars may be made in a nebula.

## NUCLEAR FUSION
A process in which lighter elements are joined together to make a heavier element; enormous amounts of energy are released in the process.

## ORBIT
The path taken by an object as it moves around another body. The Moon follows an orbit around Earth.

## PHASE
The different sunlit part of the Moon or inner planet – as seen from the Earth – as it travels around its orbit around the Earth or Sun.

## PLANET
A large object, made up mostly of rock or gas, that orbits a star.

## PLANISPHERE
A movable, circular map of the stars in the sky that can be used to show the appearance of the night sky at any given time and date.

## POLES (NORTH AND SOUTH)
The two points on a planet's surface that are furthest away from its equator.

## SATELLITE
Any object (natural or man-made) that orbits another body in space.

**SOLAR SYSTEM**
The group of eight planets, many dwarf planets and other objects orbiting the Sun.

**SPACECRAFT**
A vehicle for travel beyond Earth's atmosphere.

**SPIRAL (GALAXY)**
A galaxy with long arms that wind into a bulge at the centre. It is the most common type of galaxy.

**STAR**
A huge ball of hot gas that gives out energy from the process of nuclear fusion. Part of this energy is given out as visible light.

**STAR CLUSTER**
A collection of hundreds or thousands of stars formed together.

**SUPERGIANT**
A star that has swollen in size to tens or even hundreds of times larger than the Sun is today.

**SUPERNOVA**
A violent event that occurs when a massive star explodes.

**TELESCOPE**
A device that uses lenses or mirrors to magnify the view of distant objects.

**TEMPERATURE**
A measure of the amount of heat energy in a substance.

**TERMINATOR**
The line that divides the night (shadowed portion) and day (sunlit portion) on the Moon.

**TOTALITY**
The path on Earth's surface along which a total solar eclipse is visible.

**TRILLION**
The number equal to a million million. It is written as 1 followed by 12 zeros.

**UNIVERSE**
The huge space that contains all of time, matter and energy.

**VOLCANO**
An opening in a planet's surface through which hot liquid rock is thrown up.

**YEAR**
The length of time it takes a planet to orbit the Sun.

# Index

**Picture credits** (fc=front cover, t=top, b=bottom, l=left, r=right, c=centre)

**Alamy** Armand-Photo-CGI fc, Marc Anderson 8tr, PF-(space1) 9tr, Oliver Burston 12bl, PF-(space1) 21tr, B.A.E. Inc. 24–25c, PF-(space1) 49tr, Diego Barucco 61cr, Dennis Hallinan 63tc, Image Asset Management Ltd. 63cr, NG Images 64cr, imageBROKER 65bc, North Wind Picture Archives 71cr, PHOTOTAKE Inc. 75cl, Malcolm Park astronomy images 78c, Cultura RM 79t, Image Asset Management Ltd. 82cl, RIA Novosti 89tr, Dennis Hallinan 89l, Richard Wong 97cl, Photo Researchers 98br, NASA Archive 102br, Picture Press 105cr, shinypix 108bl, John White Photos 112–113c, Image Asset Management Ltd. 113tl

**Corbis** NASA - Hubble Heritage Team - ES/ Science Faction 4–5c, Scott Stulberg 8–9c, Tony Hallas/Science Faction 10–11c, William Radcliffe/ Science Faction 11br, STScI/NASA 13tl, Tony Hallas/Science Faction 14tr, Christie's Images 15t, STScI/NASA 29b, Roger Wood 33tr, Robert Gendler/Stocktrek Images 34bl, Tony Hallas/ Science Faction 40br, Alan Dyer, Inc/Visuals Unlimited 47tr, Stocktrek Images 51cl, 52cl, Alan Dyer, Inc/Visuals Unlimited 58–59c, 59tl, Bettmann 61tc, 62c, NASA/Roger Ressmeyer 66–67c, Christophe Lehenaff/Photononstop 67cr, NASA/Science Faction 68bc, NASA/JPL/CNP 70–71bc, NASA/Science Faction 71t, Corbis 71bl, William Radcliffe/Science Faction 72cr, Loskutnikov 72cl, William Radcliffe/Science Faction 73b, The Gallery Collection 75tr, Corbis 75b, 76–77tc, Alan Dyer, Inc/Visuals Unlimited 77br, STScI/NASA 78b, NASA GSFC/Arizona State University/Kinetikon Pictures 80–81c, Gabe Palmer 83b, Stocktrek Images 86–87c, NASA/Science Faction 88cl, Stocktrek Images 88c, Bettmann 89br, Arctic-Images 92–93c, Tony Hallas/Science Faction 94–95c, Scientifica/Visuals Unlimited 95b, Jay Pasachoff/Science Faction 97cr, Tony Hallas/ Science Faction 98–99c, Araldo de Luca 103tr, NASA 104–105t, Alan Dyer, Inc/Visuals Unlimited 105br, GIL COHEN-MAGEN/Reuters 106tr, Roger Ressmeyer/Science Faction 110tc, NASA/JPL-Caltech/UMD 110br

**Galaxy Picture Library** Robin Scagell 74cr

**Gerald Kelley** 40tr

**Getty** David Nunuk fc, Design Pics / Susan Dykstra 6–7c, malcolm park 32bl, SSPL 38c, Islamic School 43tr, Mondadori Portfolio 44bl, Visuals Unlimited 45br, Kevin Kelley 54–55c, Sovfoto 63bl, Babek Tafreshi 68–69c, DEA/G. DAGLI ORTI 69cr, NASA/Handout 75tl, SSPL 84–85ct, Steven Puetzer 94br

**NASA** JPL 74b, NASA Goddard/Arizona State University 86bl

**Science Photo Library** Science Source 23cr, Luke Dodd 35br, John Sanford 64–65c, NASA 65tl, Chris Butler 76bl, NASA 82br, Walter Pacholka, Astropics 100–101c

**Shutterstock** Claudio Divizia fc, red-feniks 3b, solarseven 4-5c, tumasia 4bl, Antony McAulay 5tl, Nik Merkulov 9cr, Michal Zduniak 8bc, Tristan3D 9bl, 10br, 11bc, Giovanni Benintende 12–13c, arigato 15br, oriontrail 18–19t, Loskutnikov 18b, ldambies 20bl, MarcelClemens 20–21bc, Loskutnikov 20cr, 21cr, Andrey Eremin 22tl, chrupka 24bl, Denis Rozhnovsky 26–27c, AlexRoz 26cr, Gautier22 27tr, studioVin 27cr, Baldas1950 28–29c, Nik Merkulov 37br, Wolfgang Kloehr 37tl, John A Davis 39cr, Nik Merkulov 47b, Naypong 51cr, Nik Merkulov 56t, Antony McAulay 56–57c, Vectomart 58bl, Gautier22 59c, David Quixley 60cr, Loskutnikov 62bc, Nik Merkulov 67tl, Loskutnikov 68c, Nik Merkulov 70c, 73t, Catmando 79br, Nik Merkulov 83tr, Quaoar 83cl, wacpan 84b, Gautier22 85bl, Suppakij1017 85br, Nik Merkulov 87tr, Viktar Malyshchyts 87br, jam4travel 90c, jwohlfeil 91tr, Loskutnikov 91bc, Quaoar 91br, Nik Merkulov 97tr, John A Davis 96–97ct, Nik Merkulov 99br, 103br, Corepics VOF 102–103c, Nik Merkulov 105c, fongfong 104br, Loskutnikov 107cr, Quaoar 107cl, Nik Merkulov 107tr, Igor Kovalchuk 108–109cl, Nik Merkulov 112cl